# TIME IS POWER

## CREATE SPACE FOR WHAT MATTERS MOST

Janice Rostron

**Time Is Power: Create Space for What Matters Most**
Published by JFnR Media
Denver, CO

Copyright © 2024 by Janice Rostron. All rights reserved.

No part of this book may be reproduced in any form or by any mechanical means, including information storage and retrieval systems without permission in writing from the publisher/author, except by a reviewer who may quote passages in a review.

All images, logos, quotes, and trademarks included in this book are subject to use according to trademark and copyright laws of the United States of America.

ISBN: 979-8-218-45017-5

SELF-HELP / Self-Management / Time Management

Cover and interior design by Asya Blue Design, copyright owned by Janice Rostron.

All rights reserved by Janice Rostron and JFnR Media.

Printed in the United States of America.

# CONTENTS

**Introduction:** You Can't Do It All! . . . . . . . . . . . . . . . . . . . . . . . . . . . . . 1

**Chapter 1:** Commit (Everything!) to Your Calendar . . . . . . . . . . . . . . . 5

**Chapter 2:** Process Your Papers . . . . . . . . . . . . . . . . . . . . . . . . . . . . . . 23

**Chapter 3:** Simplify Your Paper Files . . . . . . . . . . . . . . . . . . . . . . . . . . 31

**Chapter 4:** Maintain Your Emails . . . . . . . . . . . . . . . . . . . . . . . . . . . . . 41

**Chapter 5:** Demystify Your Digital Files . . . . . . . . . . . . . . . . . . . . . . . 51

**Chapter 6:** Delegate Your Activities Deliberately . . . . . . . . . . . . . . . . 59

**Chapter 7:** Minimize Your Junk Mail . . . . . . . . . . . . . . . . . . . . . . . . . . 69

**Chapter 8:** Diminish Your Inbox to Zero . . . . . . . . . . . . . . . . . . . . . . . 75

**Chapter 9:** Plan for Your Passwords . . . . . . . . . . . . . . . . . . . . . . . . . . . 79

**Chapter 10:** Consolidate Your Contacts . . . . . . . . . . . . . . . . . . . . . . . . 87

**Conclusion:** You Can Accomplish A Lot! . . . . . . . . . . . . . . . . . . . . . . . 93

Resources . . . . . . . . . . . . . . . . . . . . . . . . . . . . . . . . . . . . . . . . . . . . . . . . . . 95

# ACKNOWLEDGMENTS

First off, I must confess that without the worldwide pandemic in 2020, I would not have written this book. When you have an in-person home organizing business during a time that you can't enter people's homes, you either curl up into a ball in the corner *or* you create an online course and turn that course into a book. I chose the latter.

I cannot thank my husband, Craig, enough. He seems to genuinely believe that I am smart and capable and has somehow been convinced that I can do great things. I appreciate the constant reminders. And my mom, Colleen, who manages to exercise, clean the house, work in the garden, read a book, and have a cup of tea before anyone else is awake. I am just trying to keep up.

I also want to acknowledge the amazing support I have received throughout this process. Jamie Wagner and Rubecca Dalton were the first people outside my family and friends to read my original draft and made me think I was onto something here. Jim Rostron, Jacquie Paige, Dad, and all the other family members, friends, colleagues, and clients that backed my Kickstarter project made this whole endeavor financially possible. Thank you to Polly Letofsky, my publishing consultant, for holding my hand through every step, to Cheryl Jaclin Isaac, my editor, for helping to make it all make sense, and to Asya Blue Design, for making the book design look so good!

What a badass village I have built!

Finally, I am eternally grateful to *you*, the reader, for allowing me to take up a bit of your time and headspace. I do not take that privilege for granted.

# INTRODUCTION

# YOU CAN'T DO IT ALL!

*"Time is money."* —Benjamin Franklin

*"No! Time is POWER!"* —Janice Rostron

We need to stop making decisions about our time based solely on whether we will be making, saving, or spending money. Instead, we need to start viewing time itself as our most powerful asset. Throughout each stage of my life, I always focused on how the very little money I had would be affected by the decisions I made. I was proud of my accomplishments and was known to be focused and efficient in everything I did. But complete burnout forced me to learn how to prioritize more than just financial goals.

In theory, my teaching career was the highlight of my life. I was finally doing the two things I had dreamed of (and worked my butt off for) for years: teaching elementary school and playing lead guitar in a band. Awesome, right? Nope. In practice, I was wearing myself out. During that time, and I had no boundaries between my work life and my home life, no healthy habits, no self-care. By the end of 2014, I had resigned from the school district and quit the band. I was physically, mentally, and emotionally exhausted and completely and utterly burned out. When I launched my Professional Organizing business in 2015, I vowed to never let that happen again.

The year 2015 was a time of transitions. I was jumping headfirst into my new career path. I was not only learning what it meant to be a Professional Organizer, but what it meant to be a business owner. That was also the year I met my now husband. I was determined to learn from my past mistakes so I would have the time and energy for all the important pieces of my life and still have time for myself as well.

Time, unfortunately, is a finite resource, and you are doomed to burn out if you try to "do it all" in the limited time you have. There is not enough time in a day for you to build your career/business, further your education/training, work on a side hustle, clean and maintain your home, eat properly, exercise regularly, sleep well, raise children, care for an ailing loved one, bond with your friends, nurture your relationship with your partner, maintain connections with your extended family members, develop your hobbies/interests, etc., etc. Yet we try (and fail) to take it all on, every day, on our own.

If you see someone who seems to be doing it all, one of three things is happening:

1. Secretly they're sinking.
   They are completely overwhelmed and underwater, and nothing's getting done (or at least not very well).

2. Something (or someone) is suffering.
   They are putting all their time and energy into one area of their life, and another important part of their life is not getting the time and energy it deserves.

3. Someone is assisting.

They recognize their strengths, get help with their weaknesses, and drop anything that isn't truly important.

Option 3 is where I would like to get you by the end of this book. I will give you strategies to take back your time, which will then increase your power. You can't do it all, but you can accomplish *a lot* by prioritizing what's important, simplifying your systems, and delegating what you can.

After years of working as a Professional Organizer, I realized how much organization and productivity go hand in hand. You cannot stay organized when your productivity is low, and you cannot maintain your productivity when you are disorganized. This book is not designed to be read in one sitting, cover to cover. Each chapter focuses on a different area of productivity (and, of course, some organizing) that my clients often struggle with. Each topic is foundational and is meant to build upon the next, with action items at the end of each chapter so you can immediately implement what you have learned. As you read this book, take some time to build the new habits described in each chapter before moving on to the next.

So, let's get started.

Your first action item is to read Chapter 1: Commit (Everything!) to Your Calendar. As you will learn, you are more likely to accomplish something if you write it down and commit it to a specific time. This is the perfect place to begin.

Thank you for joining me on this journey to a more productive and powerful life!

## CHAPTER 1

# COMMIT (EVERYTHING!) TO YOUR CALENDAR

This is the longest chapter by design. It is the foundation for setting up a productivity system that works. How can you take back your time if you don't know where it's going in the first place?

Are you constantly overcommitting? We ~~spend~~ WASTE a lot of time rescheduling, canceling, and completely forgetting about all the activities we are "supposed" to do in a day. Let's take back your time with a simplified calendar system.

As we build our lives in this modern world, things are becoming more complicated. On top of the everyday demands of our careers, homes, partners, children, family members, friends, and hobbies, we are bombarded with more information than ever before, and it is difficult to know where and when to focus our attention. We are making two important mistakes as we try to manage our time:

1. We are focused on other people's priorities.
    We are filling our days responding to requests and committing to activities on others' schedules and deadlines. We rarely stop

to think about how important each activity is to our own lives.

2. Our obligations are often scattered across different platforms. We are juggling between paper calendars, digital calendars, passing conversations, phone calls, mail, email, texts, and messages on ever-changing apps. Relying on our memories to keep track of it all leaves us overwhelmed, disorganized, and constantly worried we are forgetting something.

## ⏱ TRUE STORY!

One day, as I finished an organizing session with a client, she asked if she could schedule the next session for the upcoming weekend.

- She picked up her phone to check her calendar. (Off to a great start!)
- We found a date and time that worked for both of us, and I added it to my calendar. (Success!)
- She paused and said, "Oh, wait, let me check if my son has a baseball game," before consulting a paper calendar hung on the refrigerator. (Derailed!)

If we hadn't been having this conversation in my client's kitchen, she would have booked the session, noticed the conflict later, and then would have had to reschedule with me, with little notice.

This last-minute rescheduling would have caused her productivity to plummet. First, she would have had to find time or interrupt another activity to contact me to reschedule. And then, she may not have gotten the services she needed on the day and time she needed them.

Simultaneously, my productivity would also have been negatively affected as I would have had to find an available date and time to accommodate her, as well as hustle to fill the now-empty slot in my work calendar. This is why businesses (including my own) charge late cancellation fees.

If you are responsible for taking your kiddos to their practices, games, or any other events or appointments, then all those dates and times should be on ONE calendar.

It is, in fact, a productive use of time to enter an entire extracurricular program into your calendar, because it will save you a ton of time and energy in the coming days/weeks/months.

## Commit to ONE Calendar

In order to avoid situations like the one my client found herself in, I want you to commit to using ONE calendar. There are many calendar options, but you can only choose ONE!

To simplify this daunting process, choose a calendar you are comfortable with. Consider how you think and work. If you are comfortable in the digital space, then a digital calendar is the way to go. If you are a paper person and prefer to physically write things down, then a paper planner is your best choice. Personally, I love digital calendars (and will point out some perks along the way), but I am not here to convert you. No productivity system will work if it goes against your natural rhythm.

If you need help selecting which digital calendar system to use, I recommend whichever program you already use and are familiar with. Unless you have an assistant, learning a completely new program may not be the best use of your time and energy. If you are a Google person and have Gmail, use the Google Calendar. If you are a Microsoft person, use the Outlook calendar. If you are an Apple person, choose iCalendar.

| The pros of using a digital calendar: | The cons of using a digital calendar: |
| --- | --- |
| • Accessibility: Digital calendars can be synced to your computer and phone so you can access them wherever you are.<br>• Shareability: Digital calendars and events can easily be shared with other people.<br>• Connectivity: Digital calendars can connect to your Maps app and get GPS directions to your destination in seconds. | • Security: Digital accounts can be hacked.<br>• Dependability: Digital accounts depend on the internet or a server, and you may lose access. |

If you prefer a paper calendar, choose a planner that has one week (ideally one day) per page, and time in 30-minute or 1-hour increments. Do not use the version with one month per page, where you only have those itty-bitty squares per day. I can guarantee that you are doing more than one thing every day! Choose a planner that has adequate space for *everything* you are doing. Shop in person, if possible, so you can get a feel for the layout and size.

| The pros of using a paper calendar: | The cons of using a paper calendar: |
|---|---|
| • Memorability: Writing things down by hand helps commit them to memory. | • Security: Paper calendars can be lost or stolen.<br><br>• Accessibility: There is only one copy, and you may not have your paper planner with you when you need it.<br><br>• Shareability: Paper calendars cannot be synced or shared.<br><br>• Productivity: Paper calendars are time-consuming to update and require a high-quality pencil and eraser. |

Be sure to create a home for your planner in your workspace. Whether you work in a traditional office, have a designated home office, or have set up shop at your dining room table, your planner needs to have a place to go. Always take it with you when you leave your workspace. You never know when you will need to refer to it throughout your day.

> ### 🕐 A NOTE ABOUT NOTEBOOKS
>
> A trusty, old-school, paper notebook can be a great tool, even for the most digital-minded. We all need a place to corral our thoughts. A notebook is a great place to take notes while on a call, jot down ideas, plan out your next project, create a shopping/packing/guest list, etc.
>
> Like the jumble of haphazard sticky notes that may or may not dot your home or office, when a notebook serves as a basin for your "brain dumps," it can quickly become unruly and unhelpful. To give it some organization, put a title (general category) and date on the top of each page so that you can quickly reference the information when needed.
>
> In general, I am not a fan of working from a to-do list. To-do lists are endless, overwhelming, and not prioritized. They are frequently setting you up to fail and to feel like you haven't accomplished enough. Why would you waste your time on something designed to make you feel bad? Instead, sort that list by priorities, and commit action items in your calendar.

## Prioritize Using Boulders, Barriers, and Building Blocks

First, determine which activities are your Boulders and prioritize them. A Boulder activity is ESSENTIAL to the health and well-being of you and your family. These activities keep your body healthy, your belly full, and a roof over your head. Your work schedule, doctor appointments, your kiddo's school schedule, and even meals are in this category.

> ### ⚡ POWER POINT!
>
> Skipping meals, regularly relying on fast food, or eating while working are unhealthy habits that can be broken by prioritizing, planning, and scheduling your meals.

standard of what true emergencies are. According to my mom, that means illness, injury, or death. I also don't recommend scrolling through social media or news apps here. This is not the time for information overload.

Create a morning Barrier and an evening Barrier and commit them to your calendar on a recurring basis, every workday. If you have children, you should schedule your Barriers before they wake up, and either before they get home from school or after they go to bed.

The final step is to determine what your Building Block activities are. A Building Block activity is designed to IMPROVE the health and well-being of you and your family. While Building Blocks are important, they are not essential to keeping a roof over your head or food on your table. Reading, extracurricular activities, classes, volunteer work, entertainment, and travel are all potential Building Block activities.

Commit these activities to your calendar last, without interfering with the Boulder and Barrier activities.

### 🕐 PRIORITIES ARE PERSONAL

Your Boulders, Barriers, and Building Blocks will be unique to you. Although I gave examples to illustrate my point, do not think of that as an exhaustive list. Your work/school demands, health, financial position, children, and other situations in your personal life will influence your priorities. Priorities will also change over time as your circumstances change.

How you prioritize reading and implementing the action items in this book is a good example of how the same activity can have a different level of importance for each person.

- If you are struggling with your productivity (e.g. forgetting important tasks at home/deadlines at work, paying bills late, neglecting your self-care, etc.), this book would be a Boulder for you.

- If you enjoy reading and/or learning productivity strategies as part of your self-care, this book would be a Barrier for you.

- If you feel good about your productivity but are looking to improve in certain areas, this book would be a Building Block for you.

I like using the image of a boulder for these activities, because they are the big, important things in life. If you try to pick up a boulder, you can't move it very far, if at all. The same goes for these activities. Boulder activities are solid in your calendar. They *have* to get done and usually on a certain day, at a certain time.

Commit every single one of these Boulder activities to your calendar, including meals. This will give you a clear, visual representation of your biggest priorities. If you are using a digital calendar, you can create recurring entries to speed up the process. If you are using a paper calendar, you will have a lot more writing to do.

The next step is to create Barriers between your work life and your home life. A Barrier activity is designed to help you simultaneously CARE for yourself while marking the beginning and end of each workday. It is a transition activity that is for your benefit only. It is not for work, it's not for your children, it's not for your partner. Barrier activities are for *you*.

> ⚡ **POWER POINT!**
>
> You (and your loved ones) want to know when your professional life ends and your personal life begins.

Use this time to schedule a self-care activity that you tend to put off, deprioritize, or typically forget about altogether. Exercise, meditation/breathing, journaling, eating a snack or having a meal at the dining table instead of at your desk, going for a walk, reading, listening to music or a podcast, or calling/texting a friend are some examples of self-care Barrier activities.

To make it a true Barrier activity between work and home, *do not* respond to work emails, texts, or missed calls, or do anything else that is work-related once you have started this activity. Yes, emergency situations arise and need to be dealt with during nonwork hours, but be sure to set the

## Create Detailed Entries

Make every entry into your calendar as detailed as possible.

- Use a verb in the title to specify exactly what needs to be done. Entering "Time Is Power" on your calendar is not helpful and the activity will most likely not get done. Instead, enter "Read *Time Is Power*, Chapter 2." This is an explicit action and is more likely to be completed.

- Enter the location of the activity.
  This could be a physical address, phone call, Zoom, etc.

- Set the beginning and end time of the activity.
  Be honest and realistic about how much time each activity will take. As you get started with this new system, schedule a slightly longer time block in your calendar for that activity. This will allow a little buffer time and you won't always feel so rushed. Use a stopwatch or timer to see how long you are spending on your regularly recurring activities and adjust accordingly. You might be surprised to learn that those "quick" activities are taking up a lot more time than you thought!

- Set all recurring activities to repeat.
  This can be done in the settings of your digital calendar or written repeatedly in your paper calendar using a high-quality, low-smudge pencil and eraser.

- Take advantage of the Notes section of your calendar.
  This section is an underutilized but extremely important part of your calendar system. Anything you need to know about that particular activity—Zoom link, supplies or materials you may need, talking points you want to cover, questions you need to ask, etc.—should be included in this section.

## Be Accountable to Your Calendar

Now that you have blocked off time on your calendar for all your priorities, you need to ensure that you spend your time accordingly, and that you are not derailed by anything of lesser importance.

- Refer to your calendar throughout the day.
  As you transition between activities, check to see if you are on track. Do not let all your planning and prioritizing go to waste.

- Keep the appointments that you make with yourself.
  You are just as important as anyone else in your calendar, so stop being a no-show for appointments with yourself.

- Make adjustments for unforeseen circumstances.
  Only allow for higher priority interruptions and disruptions to your calendar. A Building Block activity (or anything of lesser importance) should not be given priority over Boulder and Barrier activities.

- Delete, defer, or delegate lower priorities.
  If there are any activities that you realistically do not have time to do, that's OK. Remember, you can't do it all.

- Get an "accountabili-buddy" or body double.
  Ask a colleague, friend, or family member to help you stay on track by either checking in with you or working alongside you.

- Review tomorrow at the end of today.
  Check to see if there are any changes that need to be made. Gather any supplies, materials, or documents you may need to be successful tomorrow.

## Bust the Multitasking Myth

I grew up thinking that multitasking was a skill that could (and should) be developed. I was even instructed to list multitasking as a skill on my resume to impress potential employers. This thinking needs to stop. Multitasking is a myth!

Just as your body cannot be in two places at once, your brain cannot think about two things at once, and there are studies to prove it. When you think you are multitasking, you are in fact "switchtasking" (Crenshaw 2008) and slowing down your productivity. Your brain is switching back and forth between the two tasks, not doing them simultaneously. It takes time and energy to adjust from one task to another and those constant shifts are slowing down your brain's ability to retain information and your body's ability to complete a task. If you have ever forgotten something important that someone just said or made an obvious and avoidable mistake because you were working on or thinking about something else, you know this to be true. Over time, switchtasking will lead to mental exhaustion and burnout, not to mention consequences for your shoddy work or inability to recall crucial conversations.

This is why identifying your Boulder, Barrier, and Building Block activities and committing them to your calendar is so important. Time blocking in this way gives you a realistic picture of what you (and your brain) can accomplish in any given day. One of the hardest things to accept is that if you want a productive, fulfilled, and happy life, you should be *doing less* and *focusing more*.

Stop switchtasking and start focusing.

- Automate.
  Get things done without having to take time to do them. Set up your bills on autopay so the bank will pay them for you, set an out-of-office email responder so you won't have to check your email from the beach or at your friend's wedding, etc.

- Limit distractions.
  Turn off the notifications on your phone and computer while working on an important activity. Be sure to set it so that only VIPs (parents, partner, children) can disturb you and explain to them what an "emergency" means to you.

- Set a timer.
  Focus on one task until the timer goes off, or the task is complete, whichever comes first. Then reassess your time commitment for that task in the future. A visual timer like Time Timer, the timer app on your phone, or even a good old-fashioned analog clock is great for anyone that struggles with keeping track of how much time has passed.

- Allow for transition time.
  End one activity with enough time to regroup before your next activity. This means having time to put things away, collect your thoughts, gather materials for the next activity, commute, find parking, go to the restroom, eat a snack, *breathe*. You can also use these transition periods to check your phone for calls, texts, emails, and other notifications.

- Group small tasks together.
  Block time for the same activity type (phone calls, emails, errands, etc.). Bonus points if you can plan an efficient route for your errands! You can also group tasks by category (project, school, home, etc.) to keep your mind from running in more than one direction at once.

- Partner pain with pleasure.
  If there is an activity that you dislike and know you will procrastinate, drag your feet, and kick and scream before it

gets done, follow it immediately with something you love to do as a reward. So, "eat that frog" ... then eat a cookie!

- Say "no" almost every day.
  If you are asked to do something that is not a Boulder, Barrier, or Building Block activity, you are not required to do it. To ease yourself into this one, try: "No, I am not available." Full stop. No further explanation needed.

Committing everything to your calendar is not intended to create a cluttered mess that will add more stress to your life. Instead, this system will give you a tangible (or at least visual) representation of the intangible and elusive thing we call time. If the time blocks on your digital calendar start to overlap, or you are squeezing in entries where they don't fit into your paper calendar, you need to make conscious decisions to defer, delete, or delegate the lower priorities. Remember, you can't do it all.

Your time is your POWER! Don't waste it on things that are not a priority to you.

## Action Items for Chapter 1

1. Choose and commit to ONE calendar system, whether it's digital or paper.

2. Write down everything you "have" to do next week. You can print the circle map on the following page or make a copy in your notebook. This is not a typical to-do list but more of a "brain dump," so the activities will be in no particular order. (Don't forget to add reading this book and completing these action items in there!)

3. Determine your priorities by sorting those activities into Boulders, Barriers, and Building Blocks. Use the tree map format on page 21 to keep everything organized.

4. Commit everything to your calendar in order of priority: Boulders, then Barriers, then Building Blocks. Remember to create detailed entries.

    - Use a verb.
    - Enter the exact location.
    - Be realistic about the timing.
    - Set to repeat, if necessary.
    - Use the Notes section.

Please note: Some of the Building Block activities may not make it from your tree map to your calendar. That is allowed (and encouraged) so you don't overschedule yourself and try to do it all.

## Notes

TIME IS POWER

## Brain Dump Circle Map

**Week of:** _____

Write down everything you "have" to do next week.

Do not worry about the order. Simply get it out
of your head and onto the page.

**"HAVE" TO DO NEXT WEEK**

COMMIT (EVERYTHING!) TO YOUR CALENDAR

# Prioritizing Tree Map

**Week of:** _____

1. Sort the activities from your circle map into Boulders, Barriers, and Building Blocks.

2. Commit these activities to your calendar, in order of priority.

**PRIORITIES**

**MORNING BARRIER**
_____

**EVENING BARRIER**
_____

**BOULDERS**
_____
_____
_____
_____

**BUILDING BLOCKS**
_____
_____
_____
_____

## CHAPTER 2

# PROCESS YOUR PAPERS

The next four chapters are focused on the main forms of communication (paper and email) that we receive on any given day. In the age of information overload, these often become sticking points that waste our time and hinder our productivity. That is why we need to set up systems that are simple and focused on our priorities.

Are you perplexed by piles of papers? We ~~spend~~ WASTE a lot of time sorting, stacking, and searching for important papers. Let's take back your time with a simplified paper management system.

## Use the F.A.S.S.T. System

This acronym stands for File, Act, Scan, Shred, Toss. The idea behind F.A.S.S.T. is to make piles with purpose. First, you are going to sort your paperwork into five separate piles. You can use labeled papers or sticky notes to keep them organized and separated from one another.

Papers can be exhausting to process, so start with a small stack until you get the hang of it. As you sort, be sure to open all the envelopes so you know exactly what is inside. Marketing materials are often disguised as important notices and refund checks usually come in blank envelopes, so never assume anything.

Decide what needs to be done with each item by using the F.A.S.S.T. system:

- **File**: You need to keep a physical copy for future reference.

- **Act**: You need to do something.

- **Scan**: You need to keep a digital copy for future reference.

- **Shred**: You do not need it, but it contains personal information.

- **Toss**: You do not need it. Note: Of course, I mean "recycle" here, but that didn't fit nicely into my acronym!

Once you've created your five piles:

1. Create a labeled manila folder for the File, Act, and Scan piles.

2. Create a home for these folders at eye level, within arm's reach of your desktop or workspace. Action files should never be put inside a drawer or cabinet.

3. If you have a shredder, the Shred pile will go straight into your shredder. If not, schedule a time in your calendar to drop these papers off at your local shredding facility.

4. The Toss pile will go straight into your recycle bin.

## Commit Your Action Items to Your Calendar

1. Go through your Act folder and prioritize these activities as Boulders, Barriers, or Building Blocks and schedule them in that order.

2. Create a detailed entry into your calendar. Since this is a new system for you, use the Notes section of your calendar to specify that the relevant paperwork is in your Act folder.

3. Set any recurring tasks (like bills) to repeat.

4. Group small tasks either by topic (home, school, etc.) or by action (call, email, etc.). This will keep your attention focused on one thing at a time, leading to a higher success rate.

5. If you have a lot of papers relating to a specific project, they should be separated and put into their own project folder. Be sure to label the folder with the name of the project.

    a. A project consists of multiple tasks that will be completed over time. A task is a one-time action that is completed with a single action. For example, paying the insurance bill is a task; shopping around and researching different insurance companies is a project.

    b. When committing projects to your calendar, enter the next step necessary to move the project forward (e.g., Call Safeco for home and auto rates).

## Keep Papers Moving

Once an action item is completed, decide what needs to be done with the paper. Do not let it hang out in your Act folder or on your workspace. It will become clutter and lead to confusion.

- **File** it to keep the physical record.
- **Scan** it to keep the digital record.

- **Shred** it to destroy the personal information.
- **Toss** it to discard the unnecessary paper.

> ⚡ **POWER POINT!**
>
> Almost every single piece of paper in your life can be stored digitally.

## Go Paperless

To be fair, I do not expect anyone to be completely paperless as there are a few documents that we need to keep physical copies of. Important documents like Social Security cards, immigration paperwork, birth/marriage/death certificates, deeds, and any other documents that have the official government seal or watermark need to be kept in the original physical form, in a safe (fire- and waterproof) place. However, a digital copy is perfectly acceptable for most other documents.

1. Look at the papers in your Scan folder and see if you can go paperless with any of these items. This is a great place to start since you already prefer them in digital form.

2. Look at your File folder and see if you can go paperless with any of these items. Bank statements, medical records, insurance documents, most bills, and even your children's school handouts can be received in a digital format. Often, this method is preferred by most businesses and organizations.

3. Create online accounts whenever possible, using the method for password management recommended later in this book, and opt for paperless bills, statements and notices.

Your time is your POWER! Don't waste it on haphazard piles of papers.

## Action Items for Chapter 2

1. Write File, Act, Scan, Shred, and Toss on five pieces of blank paper or sticky notes.

2. Process today's mail, or any other pile of paper laying around, using the F.A.S.S.T. system.

3. Create File, Act, and Scan folders and file those papers accordingly.

4. Shred or Toss the papers you don't need.

5. Commit everything in your Act folder to your calendar. Remember to create detailed entries.

   - Use a verb.
   - Enter the exact location.
   - Be realistic about the timing.
   - Set to repeat, if necessary.
   - Use the Notes section.

## Notes

## CHAPTER 3

# SIMPLIFY YOUR PAPER FILES

D o you forget where you put those papers you now need to find? We ~~spend~~ WASTE a lot of time searching for important papers that were misfiled or never filed in the first place. Let's take back your time with this simplified paper filing system. If you dislike (or even despise) filing, this system will even work for you.

## Choose a System for Your Lifestyle

If you have large amounts of paper (more than five file boxes/drawers worth at any given time), think and work in paper, and/or have a dedicated office space, then traditional file cabinets are the way to go.

If you have a medium amount of paper (between two and five file boxes/drawers worth at any given time), prefer paper for some documents, and/or have a smaller office space, file boxes are the best option.

If you have less than two file boxes/drawers of paper, mostly think and work in the digital space, and/or have a limited (or mobile) office space, then file totes or binders will work best for you.

If you have a minimal amount of paper, are almost paperless, and/or think and work entirely in the digital space, then a simple desktop organizer or file holder is the solution for you.

## Simplify Your Setup

1. Place your file storage close to your workspace, on your dominant side. If you are right-handed, your files should be on your right side.

2. Use hanging file folders, in a single color, in each of these storage solutions. The only exception is for the desktop file holder that will just need to hold a few manila folders.

It may seem like color-coding your filing system is a mandatory unwritten rule in the "Code of the Professional Organizers." However, our goal here is *simplicity*. I have found that when my clients set up more complicated color-coded systems, these systems inevitably break down.

## ⏲ TRUE STORY!

One day, as I set up a filing system for a client in her new home, she insisted on using specific file folder colors for each category. She was a paper person and was excited about finally having a dedicated office space to store her files.

- She had purchased a large box of multicolored file folders, which included all the colors she needed. (Off to a great start!)
- I created files for her auto, home, and medical documents in the colors she requested. (Success!)
- I started to create files for her financial documents and realized she did not have enough green folders for the number of accounts she had. (Derailed!)

This color-coding mishap caused her productivity to plummet. Either she would have had to go to the store, buy another box of multicolored folders (most of which she didn't need) or an entire box of green folders (only two of which she needed). Or she would have had to "fudge it," use a yellow or blue folder that was "close enough," and hope that she remembered this fact the next time she was filing papers.

Simultaneously, my timeline for the project had to change as I had to either leave the files unfinished until the new folders were purchased, or create a slightly unorganized filing system with the wrong color folders. This is why I insist on sticking to file folders in one color.

The army-green hanging file folders may not be the most attractive, but they are easy to find at a relatively low price. Bonus points if they are made from recycled materials! They enable you to buy one box of file folders and set up your system all in one go.

## Simplify Your Paper Files

1. Create one file folder for each broad category of papers that you are keeping, and label them clearly, placing all the tabs alphabetically in the same position on the far left.

    Here are some example categories to get you started:

    - Auto: insurance, license and registration, maintenance
    - Education: certificates, diplomas, transcripts
    - Financial: expenses, income, bank/credit card/investment statements
    - Home: insurance, maintenance, warranties
    - Insurance: auto, home, life
    - Medical: EOBs/bills, prescriptions, procedures, tests
    - Retirement: 401k, 403b, investments, Social Security statements
    - Taxes: tax documents, receipts, returns
    - Work: employment documents

    One of the biggest pitfalls with paper is *over*-organizing, so always start with a big, overarching category. Documents are more likely to be misplaced if you have too many subcategories. For example: Knowing your car registration is under "Auto" is easier to remember than "Registration" or "DMV" or "Toyota" or "Prius."

2. Sort your papers into the proper folder. If every paper from a single category fits neatly into one folder, your job is done. You can now easily access those important papers in the future. It will only take a minute or two to flip through your files to find what you need, when you need it.

3. If there are too many papers to fit into one folder, then it is time to subcategorize. A good indicator of too many papers is when you can't see the label or can't close the file drawer or put the lid back on the file box.

   a. Use the F.A.S.S.T. system to declutter that category first, so you don't create files for papers that you don't even need.

   b. Create one file folder for each subcategory and label it clearly, placing the tabs alphabetically to the right of the main category tabs. For example, if the main category is Banking, the subcategories are the individual accounts, alphabetized by bank.

*An example of an organized file drawer*

Note: Do not stagger your file tabs. Like the color-coding dilemma, once you need to add a file between two folders that have already been set up, the system has failed. You will be forced to reposition all the tabs, or have a tab that is askew.

## Keep Files Moving

In order to maintain your paper filing system, you need to keep things moving. You don't want papers to pile up, and you don't want your file cabinet/box to overflow. I recommend reviewing your files annually. There is something cathartic about decluttering your files at the end of a year, or the beginning of a new year, to see how much things have changed (or stayed the same). This is also the ideal time from a financial point of view. You can pull out last year's financial documents to prepare for the upcoming tax filing. In the process, determine which files are still active and which can be archived.

Active files contain documents that you need to access regularly or are related to your current life. They should be stored in the most accessible location, within arm's reach, in your workspace.

Archive files contain older documents that need to be kept for financial, legal, or personal reasons. These can be moved out of the space, into a less-accessible location. Be sure to declutter first.

Not every Active file deserves to be kept as an Archive file. Ask yourself: "Who is going to come looking for this?" Outside of your family, financial, legal, and medical histories, most of the documents from your past can be tossed or shredded. Be sure to ask your accountant or attorney how long you need to keep financial and legal records. It's often not as long as you think.

Pull out the Archive files, put them in a new file folder, and put those folders in a file box to be stored elsewhere. Manila folders work well here. Be sure to label each folder as well as the box itself. This box can be stored up high or down low in a closet, storage unit, garage, attic, or basement.

If there are extreme temperature changes or exposure to critters in the space, opt for plastic, weatherproof boxes.

Your time is your POWER! Don't waste it on filing papers you don't need.

## Action Items for Chapter 3

1. Choose a file storage system that works for your needs.

2. Pull out the File folder that you created and sort the documents into broad categories.

3. Create file folders for each category. Be sure to label and alphabetize them.

4. File the documents into the appropriate folders.

## Notes

## CHAPTER 4

# MAINTAIN YOUR EMAILS

Are you inundated with emails? We ~~spend~~ WASTE a lot of time skimming, reading, searching for, and responding to emails. Let's take back that time with a simplified email maintenance system. Think of emails the same way you think about mail in your physical mailbox. Just like you don't leave *all* your mail in your mailbox and only take out the bills and cards that you need, you shouldn't be leaving *all* your emails in your inbox. Emails require a designated system for getting rid of what you don't want or need, and prioritizing any actions you need to take.

## Use the 6Ds System

1. Start at the top of your email inbox and work your way down.

2. Try to get through today's emails in the first sitting. It is important not to skim or skip around. This may seem tedious and unnecessary, but it will become more efficient once the system is set up and you are familiar with the steps.

3. Use the 6 Ds to determine which action you need to take with each email.

- **Do**: Reply right now.
  If you can respond to an email in one or two sentences, or there is a quick (less than a minute) action required, just do it now and get it out of the way.

- **Defer**: Act on later.
  If an email requires a longer response or necessitates you performing a task (go to an appointment, fill out a form, make a phone call, etc.), defer these emails to a later time when you can take planned and scheduled action.

  - Create an *Act folder in your email program and move all deferred emails into that folder. This folder will be used similarly to the physical Act folder in your workspace. All of the emails you need to act on will be in one place. This is an important step, but difficult for many people to implement. We have become so used to keeping emails in our inboxes that we are afraid if we move something out, it will be forgotten forever. You will thank me when you are working on your action items and they are not being buried by new emails in your inbox.

- **Delegate**: Forward to others.
  If an email needs action but can or should be completed by someone else, forward it along and get it off your plate. Remember, you can't do it all.

- **Digitally File**: Save the attachments.
  If an email has attachments that you may need to

reference in the future, save them on your computer or in your cloud service. We are trying to head toward a more paperless life, so avoid printing unless absolutely necessary.

- **Document**: File the email.
  If an email is needed for future reference, move it to the appropriate email folder.

- **Delete**: Eliminate the unnecessary.
  If you don't need an email now and won't in the future, delete it. Just like when you went through your papers and some things went straight into the recycle bin, don't be afraid to get as many unwanted emails out of your inbox as possible.

> ### ⚡ POWER POINT!
> Using the * (or any other special character) at the beginning of a digital file/folder name will keep it at the top of the list alphabetically.

## Commit Your Action Items to Your Calendar

1. Go through your *Act folder and prioritize these activities as Boulders, Barriers, or Building Blocks and schedule them in that order.

2. Create a detailed entry into your calendar.

- Use a verb.
- Enter the exact location.
- Be realistic about the timing.
- Set to repeat, if necessary.
- Use the Notes section to specify that the relevant information is in your *Act email folder. This will help you become accustomed to a new system.

3. Group small tasks either by topic (home, school, etc.) or by action (call, email, etc.). This will keep your attention focused on one thing at a time, leading to a higher completion rate.

4. If you have a lot of emails relating to a specific project, they should be separated and put into their own project folder. Be sure to label the folder with the name of the project and place it as a subfolder in *Act.

## Simplify Your Email Folders

Create one email folder (Google calls them labels) for each broad category of emails that you are keeping. Similar to our physical paper folders, this will keep important emails organized for easy access in the future.

The setup process depends on which email program you use. Technology is constantly evolving, but here are a few examples of how to set up email folders as of the date of this publication.

- Apple Mail: Mailbox menu > New Mailbox
- Gmail: Label icon > Create New
- Yahoo Mail: Move menu > Create New Folder

- Outlook: Move To menu>New Folder

To keep your system simple and consistent, create one file folder for each broad category of emails, starting with the exact same categories from your paper files. That way, your brain only has to think about one category, regardless of whether you are looking at papers or emails. Since emails don't take up physical space, are searchable by keyword, and can be sorted by date or sender, subfolders may not be needed.

- Auto: insurance, license and registration, maintenance
- Education: certificates, diplomas, transcripts
- Financial: expenses, income, bank/credit card/investment statements
- Home: insurance, maintenance, warranties
- Insurance: auto, home, life
- Medical: EOBs/bills, prescriptions, procedures, tests
- Retirement: 401k, 403b, investments, Social Security statements
- Taxes: tax documents, receipts, returns
- Work: employment documents

## Keep Emails Moving

Just like paper, emails need to keep moving. Do not let them hang out in your *Act folder or in your inbox. They will become clutter and lead to confusion. Once you have replied, completed the action, forwarded the email, or saved the attachments, decide what needs to be done with that email.

- Delete the emails that are no longer necessary or are obsolete.
- Document the emails you need for future reference.

Your time is your POWER! Don't waste it on emails you don't need.

# Action Items for Chapter 4

1. Make a print or digital copy of the 6 Ds and keep it at your workspace or on your computer desktop.

2. Maintain today's emails using the 6 Ds:

    - Do

    - Defer

    - Delegate

    - Digitally File

    - Document

    - Delete

3. Create an *Act folder and folders for other categories, as needed.

4. Commit everything in your *Act folder to your calendar.

    - Use a verb.

    - Enter the exact location.

    - Be realistic about the timing.

    - Set to repeat, if necessary.

    - Use the Notes section.

# Notes

## The 6 Ds for Email Maintenance

**Do:** Reply right now.

**Defer:** Act on later.

**Delegate:** Forward to others.

**Digitally File:** Save the attachments.

**Document:** File the email.

**Delete:** Eliminate the unnecessary.

# CHAPTER 5

# DEMYSTIFY YOUR DIGITAL FILES

Are you daunted by your digital files? We ~~spend~~ WASTE a lot of time every day downloading, searching for, and (re)requesting important digital documents. Let's take back that time with a simplified digital filing system.

## Choose ONE Digital Filing Program

Consider how you already think and work; usually this means using the program that is already tied to your email or calendar system. If you exclusively use Apple products, it will make the most sense to store your files in iCloud. If you lean toward Microsoft products, you may want to use OneDrive. If you prefer the Google platform, then use Google Drive. There are many, many other options such as Dropbox or Evernote. Ask yourself: Where are most of my digital files already stored (even if they are not organized)? That is a good place to start. Once you have decided on a program, be sure to download the app on your computer and on your phone. One huge advantage of digital files over paper files is that you can access them at any time, from anywhere.

## Simplify Your Digital Files

To keep your system simple and consistent, create one file folder for each broad category of digital documents, starting with the exact same categories from your paper files and emails. That way, your brain only has to think about one category, regardless of whether you are looking at papers or emails or digital files. Since digital documents don't take up physical space, are searchable by keyword, and can be sorted by name or date created, subfolders are not as necessary and should only be created if you have an abundance of documents in one category (i.e., you need to scroll more than two times to view them all).

- Auto: insurance, license and registration, maintenance
- Education: certificates, diplomas, transcripts
- Financial: expenses, income, bank/credit card/investment statements
- Home: insurance, maintenance, warranties
- Insurance: auto, home, life
- Medical: EOBs/bills, prescriptions, procedures, tests
- Retirement: 401k, 403b, investments, Social Security statements
- Taxes: tax documents, receipts, returns
- Work: employment documents

## Commit Your Action Items to Your Calendar

When you have digital documents (PDFs, spreadsheets, Word documents, etc.) that you need to act on, then you will create an *Act folder on your computer's desktop. This should be the *only* thing on the desktop. Start to think of your computer desktop as an extension of your physical workspace and declutter and organize regularly. Only the items you are actively working on should be out.

Most of the digital files requiring action came from your paper processing or email maintenance and are already in your calendar.

1. Go through your digital *Act folder and decide what type of priority these activities are (Boulder, Barrier, or Building Block).

2. Create a detailed entry into your calendar.

    - Use a verb.

    - Enter the exact location.

    - Be realistic about the timing.

    - Set to repeat, if necessary.

    - Use the Notes section to specify that the relevant paperwork is in your *Act folder on your computer desktop. This will help you become accustomed to a new system.

If you have a lot of digital documents relating to a specific project, they should be separated and put into their own project folder. Be sure to label the folder with the name of the project and place it as a subfolder to *Act.

## Keep Your Naming Consistent

If you are scanning papers to create digital documents, your scanner may allow you to rename the document. If not, or if you are saving an email attachment or digital download, be sure to open that document immediately and rename it.

- Start with the date in the YYYY-MM-DD format.

- Follow this with the document sender's name.

- Put the document title at the end.

- For example, the December 2023 bank statement you receive from Chase Bank will be named "2023-12-31 Chase Bank Statement."
  Please note: If you write the date in any other format, it will not show up chronologically and will be more difficult to find ("January" will show up after "December" and "12-01-2023" will show up before "12-31-2022").

If a folder gets too full (i.e., you have to scroll more than two times), feel free to break it up into smaller subcategories or declutter. Don't be afraid to use the delete button on digital documents as often as you use your shredder on physical documents. Even though digital spaces don't take up the physical space of a file cabinet, they do have finite capacity and will need to be upgraded (and paid for) once you have reached the limit. Don't keep what you don't need.

## Back Up Your Backup

You should be backing up your digital files to two different locations, a physical hard drive and a cloud-based program. Remember to use ONE cloud-based program (e.g., iCloud, OneDrive, Google Drive, Dropbox, Evernote) for all of your digital files. A double backup will ensure that you can access your documents in the event of a computer/hard drive failure or cloud error.

For the system to work, a consistent backup schedule is key.

## 🕒 TRUE STORY!

My personal experience demonstrates why this system is necessary, and that it works.

- When I started my business, I signed up for a Google G Suite account to store *all* of my business files. I also purchased an external hard drive and set a regular backup schedule. (Off to a great start!)

- A few years ago, for a reason still unknown to me, there was an issue with my Google sign-in. I did not have access to any of my work emails or files and I had an important document that I needed to complete. (Derailed!)

- I pulled out my external hard drive, plugged it in, and found the document that I needed. As I sat on hold while Google support solved the problem, I was able to carry on with my workday, as planned. (Success!)

This did *not* cause my productivity to plummet. I did not panic, curl into a ball in the corner, and start crying. I knew that my files were safe and secure in my second backup.

## TIME IS POWER

Make sure you sign into your cloud-based system daily and that you have ample storage space for your files.

3. Schedule regular backups onto your external hard drive.

- You can keep your external hard drive plugged into your computer and set it to continuously back up, or, at the end of the day/week/month, plug in your external hard drive and run a backup (schedule it in your calendar).

- The interval depends on how much information you are saving as digital files. If you are more of a paper person, you will naturally have fewer digital files and a weekly or monthly backup would suffice. If you are more digital, then continuous or daily backups are best.

Your time is your POWER! Don't waste it on disorganized computer files.

# Action Items for Chapter 5

1. Choose a digital file storage system.

2. Start with the Scan folder that you created in Chapter 2.

   - Sort the documents into broad categories.

   - Create the digital file folders for each category.

   - Scan the documents and save them to the appropriate digital file folder, using a consistent naming system.

3. Open the attachments from your emails that you want to digitally file.

   - Create digital file folders for each category.

   - Save them to the appropriate digital file folder, using a consistent naming system.

4. Create an *Act folder on your computer desktop.

5. Commit everything in your *Act folder to your calendar, as needed.

   - Use a verb.

   - Enter the exact location.

   - Be realistic about the timing.

   - Set to repeat, if necessary.

   - Use the Notes section.

## Notes

## CHAPTER 6

# DELEGATE YOUR ACTIVITIES DELIBERATELY

Are you in need of some assistance? (Every one of you should be answering: YES!) We ~~spend~~ WASTE a lot of time every day trying to do it all, but still don't get the important things done. I am going to circle back to the Introduction because I think it deserves to be repeated.

Your time is your most powerful asset. You are doomed if you try to "do it all" in the finite amount of time that you have. Remember, if you see someone that *seems* to be doing it all, one of three things is *actually* happening:

1. Secretly they're sinking.
   They are completely overwhelmed and underwater, and nothing's getting done (or at least not very well).

2. Something (or someone) is suffering.
   They are putting all their time and energy into one area of their life, and another important part of their life is not getting the time and energy it deserves.

3. **Someone is assisting.**
   **They recognize their strengths, get help with their weaknesses, and drop anything that isn't truly important.**

Option 3 is our goal! Modern life is difficult, and it truly takes a village to be successful.

## ⏱ TRUE STORY!

One of the many cooking shows I watch had a Q&A episode. The host is a cookbook author, the owner of a restaurant, a mother, a wife, a daughter, a sister, and a friend. An audience member asked her, "How do you do it all?" Her answer (after a small chuckle) was, "Oh, it just takes really good planning."

NOOO! I was devastated! She missed an opportunity to show the world, particularly the overextended women watching her show, just how she spends her time and how she does *not* spend her time. Yes, all the amazing things she does take really good planning, but her accomplishments are in direct proportion to her ability to delegate. She has a publisher, an editor, and a marketing team for her cookbooks. She has a staff running her restaurant. She has a production team producing her cooking show. She has a personal assistant handling many of her daily tasks. She has babysitters, family members, and friends helping with childcare. And so on, and so on, and so on.

## Build Your Village

"It's who you know" is a phrase I heard a lot growing up. At first, I dismissed it as another unattainable adage for the working class. Yet again, another privilege of the wealthy and well-connected. However, I've learned that we can *all* choose to surround ourselves with supportive people that help us make positive steps forward in life.

Looking back, my single mother did just that. She made sure to connect with neighbors and coworkers that she could rely on when she needed something, and she would never hesitate to help them in return. That support system, along with the list of chores she left for my sister and me while she was at work (the first step in delegation for any parent), allowed my overworked mom to have the time and energy to pursue an education, further her career, travel, socialize, and sit and enjoy a cup of tea.

Your goal should not be to get as many things done, in the shortest amount of time, as possible. That is efficiency, not productivity. Productivity is about getting the right things done, at the right time, with the right amount of energy. Rest, leisure, even intimacy, are all part of a productive lifestyle.

Remember to prioritize the Boulders (What is ESSENTIAL to your life?). Then focus on the Barriers (How can you CARE for yourself?). Then work in the Building Blocks (What can IMPROVE your life?). You must let everything else go ... or let someone else do it for you.

## Decide What to Delegate

First, take back some of your time by creating simple and consistent systems for those daily time-wasters we just learned about in this book. Then, acknowledge what cannot be delegated. To make it easy, those are the Barrier and (most of the) Boulder activities. Unfortunately (fortunately?), we have not yet developed a way to reap the benefits of someone else exercising, meditating, journaling, reading, eating, sleeping, or going to the doctor on our behalf. These activities are essential to your health and well-being and need to be done by you and you alone.

Your delegated tasks will be unique to you. Although I give examples to illustrate my point, do not think of that as an exhaustive list. Your priorities, family/social circle, and financial situation will influence what you delegate and who you delegate to. Delegation will also change over time, as your circumstances change.

Look at the Boulder and Building Block activities that are on your calendar (or still hanging out on your tree map) and start delegating deliberately. Use the flowchart on the following page and ask yourself:

1. Is it a priority?

2. Do I have time for it?

3. Can someone else do it?

## Delegate Deliberately

- Delegate one activity at a time and make adjustments as needed.

- Think outside the box.

  - Not everything has to be a paid service. Get your roommate, partner, or children involved in your home. Trade off with friends and family members to build a community of support.

  - When paying for services, start with ones that will help you catch up where you have fallen behind. For example, a housekeeper, an organizer (I know some great ones!), a handyperson, a laundromat with fluff-and-fold, a grocery store/restaurant with delivery, a babysitter, or a caregiver can help you regain control over your home life.

  - Get creative and have fun with the process!

- Say everything out loud.

  - Set the expectation about how and when a task should be completed. Your helpers are not mind readers.

  - Keep directions simple and consistent to create a higher level of success.

- Be OK with giving up a little control.

  - Focus on the goal of completing the task without it taking up time on *your* calendar. No one is going to do things exactly the way you would, and that's OK.

- Check in regularly.
    - Answer questions and provide guidance ... but do not take over.
- Use technology sparingly.
    - Chasing the newest app promising to make your life easier can often cost you in the time it takes to set it up, learn the features (and limitations), and keep it up to date. Most of the tech that I suggest using is standard for typical smartphones and computers. Keep it simple!

If you have committed everything to your calendar, you will literally start to see the newfound time available as you delegate. What POWER you have now! As I mentioned earlier, a personal assistant can help with many of these activities as well. College students or recent retirees often have the flexibility to do part-time personal assistant work.

I would be remiss if I didn't mention that I offer virtual productivity sessions on all the topics covered in this book, if you need support. Sign up for a free productivity consultation on my website: https://www.jfnr.net/productivity.

Your time is your POWER! Don't waste it on activities that can be done by someone else.

## Action Items for Chapter 6

1. Decide which Building Block or Boulder activities you can delegate.

2. Decide who you can delegate to.

3. Delegate the activity with simple and consistent instructions.

4. Focus your own time on a higher priority Boulder or Barrier activity.

5. Enjoy your new POWER!

# Notes

## CHAPTER 7

# MINIMIZE YOUR JUNK MAIL

Once these basic areas of productivity are part of your daily routine, there are some extra steps you can take to refine your processes. The next few chapters are focused on how to take your productivity to the next level.

Are you dumbfounded by the amount of junk mail you receive? We ~~spend~~ WASTE a lot of time every day moving junk mail from our mailbox to the recycle bin. And that's assuming that it doesn't go into our homes and get mixed up with important papers before it is later sorted and tossed. Let's take back that time with a few simple steps to minimize (even eliminate) the mail that is not important to you.

## Return to Sender

If you receive a lot of mail from a previous homeowner or tenant, print a page of "Return to Sender: Not at this address" labels and store them where you sort your mail. As soon as you receive their mail, peel off a label, put it on the envelope, and put the envelope straight back into the mailbox.

## Stop the Marketing Madness

If you are on countless, endless mailing lists, you have the right to opt out.

- For flyers and catalogs: http://dmachoice.org and https://save.com/mailing/delivery-options

- For credit card and insurance offers: http://optoutprescreen.com.

- Any other unsolicited mail: Contact them directly. Most websites will have a Contact page, and many of them have "Remove from mailing list" in the drop-down menu. If not, use the following email template:
  Dear ___,
  Please remove me from your mailing list. I am trying to reduce the amount of paper in my mailbox. My information is as follows:
  [Full name]
  [Mailing address]
  Thank you,
  [Signature]

## Get Over the Guilt

When you are faced with mail from charities (even the ones near and dear to your heart) and are struck with a sense of guilt for getting off their mailing lists, remember the following:

- All unsolicited mail is junk mail.

- Any free but unwanted gift is clutter and a waste of resources.

- Marketing materials are a drain on the budgets of nonprofits. I would rather my charitable contributions go to the actual work that they are doing rather than on the postage and printing of solicitations and free gifts.

- Add your regular charitable contributions to your calendar (as you would a bill that is due) and set it to repeat at regular intervals. This will ensure that your donations will be made, but the paper reminders will no longer be necessary.

- Contact them with kindness. If they do not have a "Remove from mailing list" option on their website, use the following email template:
Dear __,
Please remove me from your mailing list. I am trying to reduce the amount of paper in my mailbox. I will continue to donate to your amazing organization through your website. My information is as follows:
[Full name]
[Mailing address]
Thank you for all your hard work,
[Signature]

Your time is your POWER! Don't waste it on mail you don't need.

## Action Items for Chapter 7

1. Gather the junk mail that you received this week.

2. Determine what mail needs to be returned to the sender and what mailing lists you need to opt out of.

3. Create "Return to Sender" labels, if necessary.

4. Remove yourself from mailing lists using the opt out option on websites or direct emails.

5. Add your regular charitable contributions to your calendar.

    - Use a verb.

    - Enter the exact location (i.e., the organization you would like to contribute to).

    - Set to repeat.

    - Use the Notes section for the website or the folder you will store any solicitations, and the amount you intend to contribute.

## Notes

## CHAPTER 8

# DIMINISH YOUR INBOX TO ZERO

Are you irritated by the number of emails you receive? We ~~spend~~ WASTE a lot of time every day skimming through unimportant emails and searching for the few that *are* important. Let's take back that time by reducing the number of emails in your inbox down to ZERO. Yes, it is possible!

## Use the S.U.R.F. System

1. **Sort or Search**: Sort or search your inbox by sender. Your email program is defaulted to sort by date, so this will allow you to see all emails from one sender in one view. This process depends on which email program you are using. Again, technology will evolve, but here are the steps for the most popular email programs as of this publication.

    - Apple Mail: View menu > Sort by > From

    - Gmail: Search > From: [enter sender's name or email address]

- Yahoo Mail: Search>From: [enter sender's name or email address]

- Outlook: Filter drop-down menu>Sort>From

2. **Unsubscribe**: Unsubscribe from any senders that you are always deleting. This is the digital version of junk mail. Let them go.

3. **Remove**: Remove emails from your inbox as you would from your mailbox. Document (file) the emails that you need for future reference and delete the emails that you no longer need.

4. **Filter**: Create filters (Apple and Outlook call them rules) for any senders that you are always documenting into your email folders or are always delegating and forwarding to someone else. Filters/rules will automatically do this for you. This process depends on which email program you are using.

    - Apple Mail: Mail menu>Preferences>Rules icon

    - Gmail: Search>From: [enter sender's name or email address]>Create Filter button

    - Yahoo Mail: Three dots at the top of your email list>Filter messages like this…

    - Outlook: Settings menu: Mail>Rules

Over time, you will be left with an inbox with ZERO emails in it! Your time is your POWER! Don't waste it on emails you don't need.

## Action Items for Chapter 8

1. Use the S.U.R.F. system to diminish your email inbox to ZERO.

    - Sort or search
    - Unsubscribe
    - Remove
    - Filter or create rules

## Notes

# CHAPTER 9

# PLAN FOR YOUR PASSWORDS

Are you perplexed by the sheer number of passwords you need to keep track of? We ~~spend~~ WASTE a lot of time every day searching for, entering, and resetting our passwords. Though it may seem minimal, maybe just a few seconds, the time really adds up. Not only is it slowing down our productivity when we are "in the zone," it is also adding frustration to already overwhelming days. How many times have you just given up and moved on to the next task? Let's take back that time (and energy) with a simple plan for passwords.

## Keep to ONE Password Manager

The first step is to choose a password manager that you will use. There is no one right answer, so think about how you think, and how you work, on a day-to-day basis. If you think and work in mostly the digital space, then a digital password manager is the way to go. There are apps that are designed specifically to secure passwords. You can also create a spreadsheet, or you can use the apps that come standard on your phone/computer, such as Notes, Google Keep, or iCloud Keychain (although this last one doesn't have the capabilities of the apps).

| **The pros of a digital password manager:** | **The cons of a digital password manager:** |
|---|---|
| • Accessibility: Digital password managers can be synced to your computer and phone so you can access them wherever you are.<br>• Shareability: Digital passwords can easily be shared with other people.<br>• Security: Digital password managers can be password-protected.<br>• Searchability: Digital passwords can be searched for keywords. | • Security: Digital password managers can be hacked.<br>• Dependability: Digital accounts depend on the internet or a server, and you may lose access. |

On the other hand, if you think and work mostly in paper, and you prefer to handwrite, that's the system that you should use. I recommend using an address book for this because then you can still have an organized, alphabetical system. You can also use a standard notebook, but you should have some organization system, either alphabetically (one letter per page) or by category (one category per page).

| **The pros of a paper password manager:** | **The cons of a paper password manager:** |
|---|---|
| • Security: Paper password managers cannot be hacked. | • Security: Paper password managers are not password-protected and can be lost or stolen.<br>• Productivity: Paper password managers are time-consuming to update. |

## Protect Your Passwords

If you decide to use a digital system, you will need to protect your passwords ... with a password! So, not only will a hacker (or snooping family member) need the password to get into your phone/computer, but they will also need an additional password to access the password manager. A password app is designed with a master password in order to access the app. You can also password-protect a spreadsheet.

- Excel: File menu>Passwords
- Numbers: File menu>Set Password
- Google Sheets or Google Keep: Use your Google password to access
- Notes (Mac): Lock icon>Lock Note

If you decide to use a paper system, you will need to protect your passwords by storing them in a locked cabinet or drawer.

## Set Up a Secure System

You will need to set up a secure system for creating the passwords themselves. The most secure passwords are random. You can use the password generator function in your password app or Keychain. Yes, they will be difficult to remember since they'll contain a long string of letters, numbers, and special characters, but you won't have to keep them all in your head. The app will store the information and you can copy and paste straight from there. If you prefer choosing your own passwords, or you're not using a password app, then use these steps as a guide.

1. Choose a memorable word or phrase that's between 8 and 12 characters long.

2. Substitute some of the letters with capital letters, some with numbers, and some with special characters (e.g., Time Is Power: t!m3i$pow#R)

You don't want to use the same password for multiple accounts. Even if you use the same phrase to generate another password for another account, substitute different letters for different numbers and special characters. If any of your accounts are hacked, the hacker will then copy that password and try to access your other accounts. If you have unique passwords, only that one account will be compromised, and the rest will remain secure. What could have been a complete nightmare will now be a slight inconvenience.

## Create Detailed Entries

Unless you have a personal assistant, I doubt you have the time for a huge data entry project. Compiling all the sticky notes, notepads, scraps of paper, napkins, and anything else you may have scribbled your passwords on in the past and entering them into your new system is not a productive use of your time. I recommend setting it up as you go. Go about your regular day, and every time you sign into any of your existing online accounts, add that information into your password manager. Take the time now to enter a detailed entry (described below) so you won't have to search for information in the future.

- Business/organization name (alphabetized or categorized, if using a spreadsheet or notebook)

- Login web address (NOT the main home page)—will save you a few extra clicks

- Username

- Password

- Notes (account number, PIN, security questions, etc.)

Moving forward, be sure to update your password manager *every* time you create a new online account or update an expired or forgotten password. Do not skip this step or you will be back to the endless loop of forgotten passwords. Eventually you will have a complete and current list.

Your time is your POWER! Don't waste it on forgotten passwords.

## Action Items for Chapter 9

1. Choose a password manager that fits the way you think and work.

2. Make a detailed entry into your password manager every time you log into an online account.

3. Update your password manager every time you change your login information for an online account.

## Notes

## CHAPTER 10

# CONSOLIDATE YOUR CONTACTS

Are you confounded by the amount of contact information you need to keep track of? Are business cards, notebook pages, sticky notes, empty envelopes, and napkins riddled with phone numbers and email addresses piling up? We ~~spend~~ WASTE a lot of time every day receiving, losing track of, and searching for important contact information. Let's take back that time with a consolidated contact system.

### Choose ONE Contact Manager

If you live and work in the digital space, use the contact program in the system you are already familiar with. It can be a cloud-based program (iCloud, Google, Outlook, etc.), or you can create a spreadsheet and enter all your contact information there (Numbers, Google Sheets, Excel, etc.).

| The pros of a digital contact manager: | The cons of a digital contact manager: |
|---|---|
| • Accessibility: Digital contact managers can be synced to your computer and phone so you can access them wherever you are.<br><br>• Shareability: Digital contacts can easily be shared with other people.<br><br>• Security: Digital contact managers can be password-protected and backed up.<br><br>• Searchability: Digital contacts can be searched for keywords. | • Security: Digital contact managers can be hacked.<br><br>• Dependability: Digital accounts depend on the internet or a server, and you may lose access. |

If you are a paper person, then a good old-fashioned address book or notebook will work best for you. An address book will already be alphabetized and organized in a way that makes sense to you. If you use a regular notebook, I recommend creating some sort of organization system either alphabetically (one letter per page) or categorically (one category per page).

| The pros of a paper contact manager: | The cons of a paper contact manager: |
|---|---|
| • Security: Paper contact managers cannot be hacked. | • Security: Paper contact managers are not password-protected and can be lost or stolen.<br><br>• Productivity: Paper contact managers are time-consuming to update. |

## Create a Detailed Entry

Being consistent when consolidating your contacts will save you time from digging through stacks of business cards and deciphering the scribbles on those scraps of paper and napkins. If you have an assistant that can do data entry for you, delegate the task of entering all the loose contact information into your contact manager. If not, that would not be worth wasting the power of your time. Instead, moving forward, when you receive someone's contact info, immediately create a detailed entry into your contact manager with all relevant information:

- Full name and/or business name
- Phone number
- Email address
- Physical address
- Notes (any information that may help you remember why you wanted to stay connected with them—where you met, who introduced you, their profession, their company website, etc.)

You also want to organize your contacts based on how you think of them. For example, your dentist could go under the Ds for Dentist, under the letter of their first or last name, or under the letter of their business name. Also, if you are ready to contact someone you met more than a year ago, check your contact manager to make sure their contact information is up to date. Over time, you will have a contact manager complete with only current and important contact information.

Your time is your POWER! Don't waste it searching for someone's contact info.

## Action Items for Chapter 10

1. Choose ONE contact manager.

2. Create a detailed entry for every important contact you encounter.

# Notes

## CONCLUSION

# YOU CAN ACCOMPLISH A LOT!

The systems in *Time Is Power* are simple, but that doesn't mean they will be easy to implement. Celebrate progress over perfection. Realize how powerful you are when you take control of your time.

Over my years as a Professional Organizer, I have found a strong correlation between organization and productivity. You cannot stay organized when your productivity is low, and you cannot maintain your productivity when you are disorganized.

However, productivity is not about getting as much done as possible, in the shortest amount of time. It is about getting the right things done, at the right time, with the right amount of energy. I am often asked for tips on how to get more done. My response (even without knowing the inquirer's specific situation) is that they should be doing *less*, because more often than not, they are trying to do it *all*. This book contains the reasons behind, and the instructions to accomplish, that rudimentary response.

Life happens, of course, and you will need to periodically reassess how you are spending your time. However, you now have the tools to be productive no matter what is happening around you.

TIME IS POWER

You can accomplish *a lot* without doing it *all!* Prioritize what's important, simplify your systems, and delegate what you can. Your time is your most powerful asset. Start spending it on what matters most.

# RESOURCES

**Additional information to support *Time Is Power*:**
Just Focus & Reorganize, LLC (JFR) —
http://jfnr.net/productivity-resources

**Recommended reading to continue your productivity journey:**

David Allen, *Getting Things Done* (Penguin Books, 2002).

James Clear, *Atomic Habits* (Avery, 2018).

Dave Crenshaw, *The Myth of Multitasking* (Jossey-Bass Inc Pub, 2008).

Tiffany Dufu, *Drop the Ball* (Flatiron Books, 2017).

Regina F. Lark and Judith Kolberg, *Emotional Labor: Why a Woman's Work is Never Done and What To Do About It* (Independently published, 2021).

Julie Morgenstern, *Time to Parent* (Holt Paperbacks, 2018).

Brian Tracy, *Eat That Frog!* (Berrett-Koehler Publishers, 2017).

# ABOUT THE AUTHOR

Janice Rostron is a Professional Organizer and the owner/operator of Just Focus and Reorganize, LLC (JFR). She has been organizing the spaces around her for as far back as she can remember—just ask her family, friends, former roommates, and colleagues!

Janice's experience and wide range of interests have given her the ability to create and maintain a balanced lifestyle. She believes that simplicity is the key to success.

Janice started playing guitar as a shy, introverted 12-year-old. In her late twenties, she tackled her stage fright and joined a band. She has played shows throughout California and has recorded two full-length albums and one EP (during which time she earned the moniker "Janice F'n Reid" a.k.a. "JFR").

Janice received a BA in Legal Studies (with a minor in Music) from UC Berkeley and has since joined the Cal Alumni Association. GO BEARS! She then earned an MEd and a Multiple Subject teaching credential from UCLA. She worked as a public elementary school teacher for eight years before deciding to pursue a career in Professional Organizing.

Janice is an active member of the National Association of Productivity and Organizing Professionals (NAPO). She has earned NAPO Specialist Certificates in Workplace Productivity and Team Productivity. She served as the Los Angeles chapter's Treasurer for the 2016–2017 term. She was the leader of NAPO's Environmentally-Conscious Organizers special interest group for the 2020–2023 terms.

Janice is also a subscriber to the Institute for Challenging Disorganization (ICD) and has earned a Level II Chronic Disorganization Specialist Certificate.

Janice loves working one-on-one with her clients and enjoys speaking to groups about organization and productivity.

In 2022, Janice moved to Denver to grow the business ... and purchase her first home.

www.ingramcontent.com/pod-product-compliance
Lightning Source LLC
Chambersburg PA
CBHW070206100426
**42743CB00013B/3066**